Original title:
Love's Compassionate Journey

Copyright © 2024 Swan Charm
All rights reserved.

Author: Eliora Lumiste
ISBN HARDBACK: 978-9916-89-352-4
ISBN PAPERBACK: 978-9916-89-353-1
ISBN EBOOK: 978-9916-89-354-8

Hearts Entwined Along the Path

Two souls wander, side by side,
In laughter's echo, love won't hide.
Through tangled woods, they find their way,
Each step a promise, come what may.

Sunlight filters, warm and bright,
Casting shadows, love's true light.
Hands held gently, fingers lace,
On this journey, there's no race.

Moments linger, time stands still,
In heartbeat whispers, they fulfill.
With every glance, their spirits soar,
Two hearts entwined, forevermore.

A Tapestry of Gentle Touches

Softly woven, threads unite,
In tender moments, day and night.
A tapestry of whispers sweet,
Where every heartbeat finds its beat.

Caress of breeze, a feather's kiss,
In silent corners, purest bliss.
Colors blend in subtle shades,
Embracing love that never fades.

Each gentle stroke, a story told,
In patterns rich, their love unfolds.
With every touch, new dreams ignite,
A tapestry of hearts in flight.

Whispers of Kindred Souls

In silent moments, secrets share,
Two kindred souls, a bond so rare.
Whispers linger on softest sighs,
In depths of night, beneath the skies.

Dreams entwined like vines that climb,
They dance together, saving time.
Echoes of laughter float above,
In every voice, a trace of love.

Hand in hand, they journey forth,
Guided by light, true north.
Through every storm, they brave the seas,
Whispers of hope will never cease.

The Map of Our Embrace

Across the hills where memories flow,
The map of us begins to grow.
Each curve and line, a story drawn,
Guiding us from dusk to dawn.

X marks the spot where hearts collide,
In every tear, in every stride.
A journey etched in love's own ink,
Together stronger, we won't sink.

From valleys low to mountains high,
With every breath, we touch the sky.
A treasure found in every place,
The map unfolds, it's love's embrace.

Serendipitous Encounters of Grace

In the quiet of the night,
Stars whisper secrets light,
Paths cross like gentle streams,
In moments woven from dreams.

Eyes meet in a fleeting glance,
Hearts dance in a chance romance,
Words flow like honeyed song,
Reminding us where we belong.

Laughter shared under the moon,
Time slows, like a sweet tune,
Hands brush in a soft caress,
In such moments, we are blessed.

Each encounter leaves a trace,
A warmth, a fleeting embrace,
We carry these gifts so dear,
In our hearts, they reappear.

With grace, we walk this earth,
Finding joy in simple worth,
Each serendipity's embrace,
Shapes our story, fills our space.

Tracing the Lines of Shared Experience

In the lines of our laughter,
A map of dreams we gather,
Tracing paths we walked together,
Through storms and sunny weather.

Hidden stories in our eyes,
Reflections of our goodbyes,
Moments etched in warm embraces,
Time's treasure in familiar places.

Through the struggles and the strife,
We build a tapestry of life,
Each thread a bond, a shared tear,
In unity, we conquer fear.

With every lesson that we learn,
A flicker of hope will return,
In every chapter that we write,
We find the spark, we find the light.

Navigating twists of fate,
We share the love, we celebrate,
Together, we begin to see,
The beauty in our journey.

The Bridge Built by Kindness

Across the river flows a stream,
Constructed from a shared dream,
Each plank a gesture, strong and true,
A bridge connecting me to you.

Acts of kindness left behind,
A gentle touch, a heart aligned,
In every smile that lights the way,
We find the hope to face the day.

The whispers of compassion's song,
Remind us where we both belong,
Building bridges, we inspire,
With every act, igniting fire.

Through the storms, through the night,
We find our way, we find the light,
For every hand that reaches out,
Creates a world free from doubt.

Let kindness be our guiding star,
It's how we heal, it's how we are,
Together, let's create the space,
For love to thrive, for hearts to brace.

A Quest for Unconditional Embrace

In the depths of every heart,
A longing for a brand new start,
To find a love that knows no bounds,
In every silence, hope resounds.

We journey through the highs and lows,
Seeking comfort, beauty grows,
With each step, we come to see,
The power of vulnerability.

Unraveled dreams and tender wounds,
In shared shadows, hope attunes,
With open arms, we walk this road,
Embracing every heavy load.

Through trials faced and laughter shared,
An unconditional love declared,
It nurtures roots, it helps us rise,
In every touch, the spirit flies.

The quest for love, a timeless chase,
In every moment, find our place,
With hearts entwined, we'll set the pace,
To journey forth in warm embrace.

Seeds of Kindness in Every Step

In every smile, a seed is sown,
A whisper of love, never alone.
With every gesture, hope will bloom,
A brighter world dispels the gloom.

With patience warm and hands held high,
Together we'll learn to touch the sky.
For in our hearts, a garden grows,
Where kindness reigns and love bestows.

Let laughter echo through the day,
As blooms of friendship find their way.
In tiny acts, the magic flows,
In every heart, compassion glows.

Through trials faced, we lift each other,
In every soul, a caring mother.
With steps we take, let kindness lead,
A world transformed by every deed.

Together we walk, hand in hand,
Sowing kindness across the land.
In every step, a chance we find,
To plant the seeds of love, so kind.

The Unfolding Story of Us

Two souls entwined, a tale begins,
With laughter shared and playful sins.
Each chapter written, page by page,
In the book of life, we set the stage.

From first sweet glance to whispered dreams,
We navigate through life's great streams.
In every moment, love will dance,
A sacred bond, a timeless chance.

Through storms we face, we stand as one,
In darkest nights, we seek the sun.
Our story woven, threads of gold,
In every heartbeat, love's tale told.

With every challenge, we will grow,
In fields of trust, our gardens sow.
Together writing what we crave,
The unfolding story that we brave.

So let us write with hearts ablaze,
In every breath, a new phrase.
For in this journey, hand in hand,
We are the authors of this land.

Journeys Through Open Hearts

In every heart, a journey waits,
Through open doors and golden gates.
With tender steps, we navigate,
The paths of love that we create.

Each story shared, a bond we weave,
In open hearts, we learn to believe.
With every smile, a light ignites,
Guiding us through the darkest nights.

Together we seek, together we find,
The beauty in leaving fear behind.
With open hearts, we draw others near,
In unity faced, we conquer fear.

Through winding roads, we walk with grace,
Embracing life and every place.
Through joys and sorrows, we share our art,
For journeys thrive in open hearts.

So take my hand, let's journey wide,
With open hearts, we'll turn the tide.
For every step, a treasure gained,
In love's embrace, our spirits trained.

The Embrace of Kindred Spirits

In gentle whispers, we connect,
A bond unspoken, deep respect.
With kindred spirits, we take flight,
Illuminated by shared light.

Through trials faced, we stand as one,
In laughter's echo, we have fun.
In every moment, joy aligns,
With spirits mingling, love entwines.

From different paths, we come together,
In shared dreams, we brave the weather.
With hearts attuned, we feel the glow,
Of friendships woven, strong and slow.

In twilight's glow, stories unfold,
Of kindred spirits, brave and bold.
Through every hug, our souls ignite,
In unity found, we share the night.

So hold my hand, let's journey far,
Together shining, like a star.
In the embrace of those we choose,
Kindred spirits, we never lose.

Poetic Steps toward Connection

In the quiet of the night, we find our way,
Every whispered word, a gentle sway.
Hearts open wide, like the skies above,
Each step we take, a dance of love.

With hands to hold and eyes that see,
We bridge the gaps, you and me.
Moments fleeting, yet they remain,
Bonded in joy, softened by pain.

Our laughter sings, a soothing balm,
In shared stories, we find our calm.
Through valleys deep and peaks so high,
Together we journey, you and I.

Listen closely, the world does call,
Echoes of truth in a whispered thrall.
Every heartbeat syncs, a rhythm true,
In connection's embrace, we renew.

So take my hand, let's walk this line,
With every step, our spirits entwine.
In the tapestry of life, we weave,
A connection born, in hearts, we believe.

A Way to Live

In morning's light, we start anew,
With open hearts, to dreams we'll pursue.
Each sunrise brings a chance to be,
Alive with hope, in harmony.

Embrace the moments, fleeting and rare,
With kindness given, a world to share.
Small acts of grace, like seeds we sow,
In the garden of life, watch love grow.

Let laughter ring, let joy abound,
In simple pleasures, fulfillment is found.
Hold tightly to those who bring you peace,
In every connection, let worries cease.

Challenge the shadows, embrace the light,
With courage kindled, our spirits take flight.
In every heartbeat, a rhythm divine,
A way to live, where stars align.

So dance through life, let your heart lead,
Nurture your soul, plant every seed.
In the embrace of love, find what's true,
A way to live, just me and you.

A Way to Care

In a world that sometimes feels cold,
Let warmth and kindness be our gold.
With gentle words, we soothe the pain,
In acts of love, our courage gained.

Listen closely, hear the unspoken,
In every tear, a heart's token.
With open arms, we greet the day,
Showing compassion, lighting the way.

When shadows loom, stand hand in hand,
In unity, together we'll stand.
Every smile shared, a healing grace,
In the dance of life, we find our place.

Support each other through thick and thin,
In every struggle, we find strength within.
With empathy deep, let understanding flow,
A way to care is the path we'll know.

So let's build bridges, tear down the walls,
With love as our guide, when duty calls.
In a tapestry rich, woven with care,
Our hearts will flourish, our spirits laid bare.

A Voyage Through Compassionate Waters

We sail upon the gentle sea,
Where hearts unite in harmony.
Each wave a whisper, soft and true,
A bond that's formed in shades of blue.

Together we face the rising tide,
With every storm, there's love inside.
The compass points to shores unknown,
Yet we are never truly alone.

Our vessel carries dreams and fears,
Navigating through laughter and tears.
In each other's eyes, we find our way,
Through compassionate waters, we shall stay.

The Light of Empathetic Gazes

In a world where shadows often loom,
We seek the light that helps us bloom.
An empathetic gaze can heal,
Transforming pain to strength we feel.

With every look, a bridge is built,
Erasing doubt, dissolving guilt.
Through silence shared and warmth embraced,
We find a sanctuary, a sacred place.

The light shines bright in darkest night,
Two souls entwined in pure delight.
In understanding, deep and wide,
We walk together, side by side.

Hand in Hand Through Life's Mosaic

Life's mosaic is vast and grand,
With colors bright, we join our hand.
Each piece a story, rich and rare,
Together we weave a tapestry in air.

Through highs and lows, we navigate,
Trusting in love, our shared fate.
Side by side in bright array,
We face each dawn, we greet each day.

In laughter's echo, our spirits soar,
Hand in hand, we explore and more.
Every moment a brushstroke fine,
Creating memories, yours and mine.

Beneath the Canopy of Kindness

Beneath a canopy lush and green,
We find a world serene, unseen.
Where kindness rains like gentle drops,
And love's embrace never stops.

In shadows cool, our hearts align,
With whispers soft, our spirits shine.
Each act of care a feathered wing,
Together we rise, together we sing

In this haven, we plant our dreams,
Nurtured by hope and gentle beams.
Through storms and sun, we proudly stand,
Beneath the sacred, kind command.

The Dance of Empathetic Hearts

In the rhythm of life's gentle sway,
Two souls connect in bright array.
With every step, they learn and grow,
A garden of feelings starts to show.

In the silence, they hear the call,
Echoing softly, a love enthralled.
Through laughter and tears, they intertwine,
Crafting a bond, resilient and fine.

With open minds and tender grace,
They find their strength in each embrace.
A dance that weaves through joy and pain,
In the depths of hearts, love will remain.

With every glance, the world ignites,
Creating warmth in the coldest nights.
Two kindred spirits, hand in hand,
Together they flourish, together they stand.

In this dance, they discover the art,
Of building bridges, heart to heart.
In every beat, a promise clear,
A world transformed when love is near.

Paths Woven with Kindness

In every step, a kindness shared,
A gentle word, a heart declared.
Through busy streets, and quiet lanes,
Compassion blooms where love remains.

With outstretched hands, they greet the day,
Carving joy in their own way.
From stranger's smile to friend's embrace,
In every gesture, a sacred space.

As rivers flow, so flows their grace,
Through trials faced, a warm embrace.
A tapestry rich with stories spun,
Of all they've faced, together as one.

In laughter shared and burdens less,
They find the strength to truly bless.
With every act, their spirits rise,
A symphony of heartfelt ties.

In the garden of kindness, hearts will bloom,
Nurtured by love, dispelling gloom.
Paths of gold where all can tread,
In unity's light, all fears are shed.

Lanterns Guiding Through Shadows

In the darkness, lanterns gleam,
Lighting paths that softly beam.
Each flicker tells a story bright,
Of hope unfurling in the night.

Through the fog and the heavy mist,
They cast a glow, and hearts persist.
With every flick, despair takes flight,
Guiding souls toward the light.

In whispered thoughts, shadows loom,
Yet lanterns break the silent gloom.
Together, they navigate the way,
With courage found in dawn's first ray.

With every step, fears gently fade,
In the warmth of love, fears are laid.
Lighting the journey, hand in hand,
Building a bridge to a promised land.

In the night's embrace, they find their song,
In every heartbeat, where they belong.
With lanterns raised, they face the stars,
Together they shine, with no more scars.

The Symphony of Shared Breath

In the stillness, a breath unfolds,
An orchestra of hearts, love bold.
Each exhale, a note, pure and clear,
Binding them close, forever near.

With every rhythm, a dance is made,
In the silence where dreams cascade.
The music flows through the open air,
A symphony woven, sweet and rare.

In moments shared, a harmony grows,
Through whispered secrets and soft echoes.
Their laughter rings like chimes on high,
Creating melodies that never die.

With every heartbeat, the world aligns,
In sacred space, their spirit shines.
A masterpiece crafted, gentle and true,
In the symphony, they find the view.

In the embrace where hopes collide,
Together they journey, side by side.
A chorus of souls, forever entwined,
In this love song, true peace they find.

The Trail of Warm Connections

On paths where kindness dwells,
Our stories intertwine,
With every step, a memory tells,
A bond that's pure, divine.

In whispers shared beneath the trees,
The laughter finds its way,
Through gentle winds, our hearts at ease,
Creating bright array.

Together we explore the trails,
With trust as our embrace,
Through winds and storms, love never fails,
In every sacred space.

Each moment shared, a treasured gift,
Life's journey side by side,
In every heart, a silent lift,
With joy as our guide.

As twilight falls, we gather near,
In warmth, we find our place,
With open hearts, we hold so dear,
Together, love's sweet grace.

Echoes of Caring Hearts

In shadows cast by gentle light,
We find our voices blend,
In every echo, hope takes flight,
As hearts begin to mend.

A tapestry of stories spun,
In laughter, tears, and sighs,
Together we have just begun,
To reach for summer skies.

Each caring word a soothing balm,
That wraps us in its glow,
In quiet times, we find our calm,
A love that's pure and slow.

Through trials faced, we stand as one,
With every challenge met,
In echoes soft, our hearts are spun,
A bond we won't forget.

As stars appear in evening's grace,
We cherish what we've found,
In the rhythm of this sacred space,
Our caring hearts abound.

Unfolding the Garden of Us

Within our hearts, a garden grows,
With petals soft and bright,
In every seed, our love still flows,
In morning's golden light.

We tend the blooms with gentle hands,
And nurture every dream,
In trust, united, like the sands,
We flourish as a team.

Each flower speaks of moments shared,
Of laughter, tears, and grace,
In fragrant air, we're unprepared,
For beauty's warm embrace.

As seasons change, so do we bloom,
Embracing every kiss,
In colors rich and sweet perfume,
We find our perfect bliss.

Together, let our garden thrive,
Through storms and sunny days,
In love's embrace, we come alive,
In countless, loving ways.

The Symphony of Shared Laughter

In every giggle, joy takes flight,
A symphony so pure,
In harmonies that feel so right,
Our laughter is the cure.

With every joke, the world ignites,
In playful, sweet refrain,
Through shared delight, our spirit bright,
We dance in joyful rain.

Each chuckle builds a bridge so wide,
Connecting hearts tonight,
In moments shared, we will confide,
Our burdens feel so light.

As time unfolds, the music plays,
In rhythms of our souls,
Through every smile, love's magic stays,
And fills our deepest roles.

Together, we create a song,
In notes of pure delight,
In shared laughter, we all belong,
Our hearts are shining bright.

A Dance of Hearts in Transit

In the twilight's gentle embrace,
Two souls find their dance,
Spinning dreams in quiet grace,
Together in this fleeting chance.

Hands entwined, they glide as one,
Whispers soft, a lingering sigh,
The rhythm of hearts, just begun,
As moments pass, they learn to fly.

With every step, a new delight,
In shadows cast by soft moonlight,
Each laughter shared, a spark ignites,
Within their hearts, no room for fright.

The music rises, swirls around,
In perfect time, they feel the sound,
Lost in a world where love is found,
In transit, where their hopes abound.

Yet time, like tides, must ebb and flow,
As journeys call them far away,
But in their hearts, the seeds will grow,
A dance of love that's here to stay.

Melodies of Understanding

In the stillness, words collide,
And silence speaks of shared truths,
With every note, their hearts confide,
In melodies that bridge their youths.

A gentle strum, a tender hum,
Resonates through weary bones,
With each refrain, they find their sum,
In songs that soothe, where love condones.

Through dissonance, they seek to mend,
A harmony born of the pain,
In every gap, they learn to blend,
Creating peace amidst the strain.

The echoes of their laughter rise,
Filling spaces once so bare,
As wisdom dances in their eyes,
In understanding's warm repair.

Together, they can face the night,
These melodies, their guiding stars,
In every note, a path so bright,
Unraveled dreams beneath the scars.

A Foray into Forgiveness

In the chamber of the heart,
Grudges linger, cold as stone,
Yet tender hands can play their part,
To break the silence, create a tone.

With every breath, the courage grows,
To let the past just drift away,
For in forgiveness, truth bestows,
A brighter dawn, a new array.

Each step may tremble, but they'll tread,
On paths where wounds once drew the line,
Their spirits rise, no longer fed,
By memories that seek to bind.

Through misty valleys, they will roam,
With hearts as open as the sky,
In sharing pains, they find a home,
And learn that love can never die.

The journey's long, yet worth the strive,
For every scar can teach them grace,
In forgiveness, both will thrive,
Embracing each other's rightful place.

Gentle Steps Beneath Starlit Skies

Underneath the vast expanse,
They wander in the midnight glow,
With every heartbeat, every glance,
Their souls entangle, ebb and flow.

Soft whispers dance among the trees,
As secrets shared ignite the night,
In nature's quilt, they find their ease,
And every star becomes their light.

The world may fade, but dreams ignite,
With gentle steps on softest ground,
In this embrace, all feels so right,
As starlit vows in silence sound.

Together, they unfold the night,
With laughter high and spirits free,
In every twinkle, pure delight,
Their hearts a song, eternally.

As dawn approaches, shadows wane,
But memories shine like morning dew,
In every moment, love remains,
A testament to journeys new.

Wings of Serenity and Care

In whispers soft, the breezes flow,
With gentle grace, where calmness sow.
We lift our hearts, like birds on high,
In unity, we learn to fly.

A tranquil sky, painted blue,
With every breath, our spirits renew.
In tender folds of love we hide,
Through trials faced, we'll stand with pride.

Each moment shared, a bond we weave,
In fields of hope, we shall believe.
For in each heart, a fire glows,
With wings of care, our friendship grows.

In quiet times, we find our peace,
Where burdens light, and worries cease.
Together we embrace the fate,
With wings of serenity, we wait.

Through storms that come, we'll not despair,
For in our hearts, we find our share.
In harmony, our dreams will soar,
With wings of love, we'll ever more.

Heartbeats Beneath the Same Canopy

Under the shade, where sunlight fades,
Two hearts beat strong, in gentle cascades.
A rhythm shared, a pulse so near,
In whispered breaths, the world disappears.

With every laugh, a memory blooms,
In this sacred space, all doubt consumes.
Through seasons bright, together we roam,
In nature's arms, we find our home.

With every story, our souls entwine,
In the quiet woods, we sip the wine.
Of friendship rich and love so true,
Beneath the canopy, me and you.

As shadows grow and twilight calls,
In the starlit sky, our laughter falls.
In harmony, our spirits rise,
Two heartbeats strong, beneath the skies.

For in this bond, we find the way,
Together in night, together in day.
With hearts aligned, forever free,
We thrive as one, beneath this tree.

Sails of Companionship on Life's Sea

Upon the waves, we set our course,
With sails unfurled, we feel the force.
Through tempest strong and waters wide,
Together, we shall turn the tide.

In shared adventures, we laugh and cheer,
Embracing challenges without fear.
With every gust, our spirits rise,
As kinship shines like sunlit skies.

A journey long, with maps unrolled,
In tales of old, our dreams unfold.
In every harbor, a story waits,
With sails of trust, we navigate.

The moon our guide, the stars our light,
Through darkest times, we hold on tight.
With hearts ablaze, our sails will hum,
To life's vast sea, we both succumb.

For in this life, we chart and steer,
With voices raised, we persevere.
Sails of companionship, bold and free,
Together we'll weather whatever may be.

Kaleidoscope of Shared Moments

In colors bright, our laughter plays,
Like dance of light on sunny days.
A tapestry of memories spun,
In every thread, two lives as one.

With every glance, a story told,
In silent whispers, hearts unfold.
Through seasons change, we shift and sway,
In a kaleidoscope, forever stay.

From humble starts, our journey grows,
In every shadow, a flower shows.
Together we paint, with vibrant hues,
The masterpiece of me and you.

As time flows on, with gentle ease,
In cherished moments, we find our peace.
With every heartbeat, love ignites,
In kaleidoscope, our souls take flight.

For in each color, there lies a spark,
Illuminating paths through the dark.
In life's embrace, we'll ever stand,
In shared moments, hand in hand.

An Odyssey of Gentle Hearts

Upon the waves of quiet night,
We sail our dreams in soft moonlight.
With every whisper, hope ignites,
Two gentle souls, in love's delight.

Each breath a journey, hand in hand,
Through seas of time, we understand.
In laughter's echo, doubts fade away,
Together we dance, come what may.

Stars guide our way, shining so bright,
With every heartbeat, love takes flight.
In harmony, we find our song,
With gentle hearts, we both belong.

The winds may howl, the storms may rage,
But love's embrace will be our gauge.
Through tempests fierce, our bond stays true,
An odyssey born, just me and you.

In every tide, our tale unfolds,
A tapestry of dreams retold.
As dawn approaches, fears dissolve,
In gentle hearts, our world revolves.

In the Arms of Silent Deliverance

In shadows deep, where whispers dwell,
We find a peace that words can't tell.
With every sigh, our spirits blend,
In silent grace, we find our mend.

The night enfolds with tender care,
A sacred bond, a silent prayer.
In heartbeats soft, our solace found,
Together lost, forever bound.

Through trials faced and sorrows shared,
A refuge strong, we both have dared.
In gentle light, we seek the dawn,
With every moment, fears are gone.

In stillness, joy begins to swell,
A love that echoes, casts a spell.
With open arms, the world does cease,
In silent deliverance, we find peace.

Each heartbeat whispers love's sweet tune,
With every glance, we touch the moon.
In the arms of night, dreams take flight,
Together we soar, hearts burning bright.

The Lighthouses of Our Hearts

When shadows fall and night sets in,
Your love shines bright, where I begin.
With every beacon, guiding light,
Through darkest storms, you spark my fight.

In weathered whispers, tales unfold,
Of dreams embraced, of stories told.
Each moment shared, a guiding star,
We navigate, no matter how far.

The waves may crash, the winds may howl,
Yet in your gaze, I find my prowl.
With every pulse, my heart you hold,
A lighthouse strong, a love so bold.

Together facing the raging sea,
In every struggle, I find the key.
Your light, a promise, steadfast and true,
The lighthouses of hearts, me and you.

Through storms and tides, our journey flows,
In every challenge, love only grows.
A shining path, forever impart,
The lighthouses, forever in heart.

Traces of Affection on Winding Roads

On winding roads, where footsteps tread,
With each embrace, words left unsaid.
In whispers soft, through twists and turns,
The fire of love eternally burns.

Beneath the stars, our secrets bloom,
In silent nights, our hearts consume.
With every mile, we find our place,
Traces of affection, a warm embrace

Through valleys deep and mountains high,
Our love's a journey, we can't deny.
In tangled paths, we chart our way,
With laughter's echo, come what may.

From dawn to dusk, each moment shared,
In every challenge, we have dared.
With open hearts, we share the load,
On winding roads, love has bestowed.

Each turn reveals what we hold dear,
In every glance, the world is clear.
Traces of affection forged so fine,
On winding roads, your heart is mine.

Finding Solace in Togetherness

In the quiet moments, we find peace,
Hand in hand, our worries cease.
A shared smile lights up the gloom,
Together we create a cozy room.

Laughter dances in the air,
Filling spaces, everywhere.
In each heartbeat, love's embrace,
Togetherness finds a perfect place.

Through storms that may come and go,
United, our strength will surely grow.
With gentle whispers, hearts align,
In every touch, your soul meets mine.

The world fades, but we remain,
In each other, we share the pain.
Through trials, together we soar,
In our bond, we find much more.

As day turns into night's embrace,
Together we've built a sacred space.
Endless moments, love's sweet song,
In togetherness, we both belong.

A Narrative Woven with Care

Threads of time, stitched with grace,
Every memory finds its place.
In stories told, our hearts entwine,
A tapestry of yours and mine.

Every whisper, soft and clear,
Builds a bridge that draws us near.
Each laughter shared, an intricate part,
Woven gently into the heart.

In the pages of the past,
Moments cherished, always last.
Through every twist and every turn,
Together we endlessly learn.

With each chapter that we write,
A dance of shadows and of light.
In this narrative, joy and sorrow,
We find the strength to face tomorrow.

So let's pen our tale with care,
In every word, a wish, a prayer.
In every silence, a voice is heard,
Our story flourishes, uncurbed.

Vows Whispered Among the Stars

Underneath the evening sky,
With the stars, our dreams apply.
Softly spoken, vows ascend,
In this moment, time shall bend.

Hearts aligned, pulse in sync,
In love's embrace, we seldom think.
Promises made in moonlight's glow,
In every glimmer, our feelings show.

Minds entwined, futures bright,
Guided solely by love's light.
Every star a tale revealed,
A universe, our hearts are sealed.

With each wish upon a star,
Our bond deepens, near or far.
In silence shared, our spirits soar,
With whispered vows, forevermore.

As constellations find their path,
In every moment, love's sweet math.
Bound by fate, hand in hand,
Vows amidst the stars, we stand.

Embracing the Essential: A Tale of Togetherness

In simplicity, we find our way,
Together, at the close of day.
Shared moments, soft and bright,
A tapestry woven in pure light.

The essential joys that often glide,
Are found in love, and here we bide.
In laughter's ring, in each caress,
Together, we embrace the blessedness.

Through shifting times, and endless roads,
In each other, we share the loads.
Heart to heart, we journey on,
In togetherness, we've truly grown strong.

In every challenge that we face,
We find strength, we find grace.
Simple joys, a knowing glance,
In our love, we take our chance.

Let's savor life's essential art,
Together, never far apart.
In each heartbeat, our story flows,
In togetherness, our love shows.

The Palette of Tender Moments

Brush strokes of laughter,
Colors of sweet delight.
Each moment a canvas,
Painted in soft twilight.

Whispers of warm breezes,
Gentle touches of grace.
Memories like soft petals,
Fading at their own pace.

Frames of shared silence,
Every glance a soft spark.
In the glow of the evening,
Love ignites in the dark.

Through the colors of heartache,
We learn to blend and mend.
Each shade tells a story,
Of love that will not end.

With each stroke of kindness,
We create our own tune.
In the gallery of living,
Moments forever bloom.

Chasing Shadows of Affection

Beneath the moon's soft glow,
We wander hand in hand.
Chasing shadows of longing,
In a twilight land.

Every whisper a promise,
Every touch a soft breeze.
In the dance of our shadows,
We find our heart's ease.

Fleeting yet eternal,
These moments come alive.
Through the labyrinth of dreams,
Together we strive.

In the twilight's embrace,
We linger, we sigh.
Chasing shadows of affection,
As the stars fill the sky.

With each fleeting heartbeat,
We craft our own lore.
In the chase of our shadows,
We always want more.

A Bridge over Emotional Waters

When storms cloud the horizon,
And the waves start to rise,
A bridge made of courage,
Connects our weary sighs.

Each plank whispers comfort,
Each rail shines with care.
Through turbulent seasons,
We find solace to share.

The waters may tremble,
And the currents may sway.
Yet on this strong bridge,
We'll never lose our way.

With every step forward,
We leave fears behind.
Hand in hand we travel,
With a love intertwined.

Through valleys and mountains,
This bridge will not break.
Together we'll wander,
For our hearts are awake.

The Seasons of Compassionate Connection

In spring, we find promise,
With blossoms in the air.
The warmth of our laughter,
A bond beyond compare.

Summer whispers softly,
Underneath the bright sun.
Hand in hand we're dancing,
Two souls become one.

Autumn brings reflection,
With leaves that gently fall.
In the quiet moments,
We hear the heart's call.

Winter wraps us closely,
In blankets of white snow.
In the fires of our hearts,
Compassion starts to glow.

Through every changing season,
Our connection will thrive.
In the dance of existence,
Together we're alive.

The Rhythm of Kindred Spirits

In whispers soft, our laughter we share,
Threads of connection in the tender air.
With every heartbeat, an unspoken song,
Together we dance, where we both belong.

Through sunlit days and starry nights,
We find our way, guided by the lights.
A bond unbroken, woven so tight,
In the rhythm of souls, everything feels right.

The silent glances, the knowing smiles,
In moments of stillness, we walk for miles.
Our hearts in sync, like waves on the shore,
In the rhythm of kindness, we ask for more.

Embracing the journey, each step we take,
Building a friendship that never will break.
In the garden of trust, we plant our dreams,
Where kindred spirits flow like gentle streams.

Through stormy weather and skies of blue,
With every challenge, we start anew.
In the rhythm of life, hand in hand we strive,
Together forever, we truly survive.

Pages of a Story Yet Unwritten

In every moment, a chapter begins,
Where hopes and dreams spark like distant twins.
With ink of intention, we write our fate,
The pages await for love to create.

With every heartbeat, the story unfolds,
Tales of adventure, of brave souls bold.
In whispers of wonder, secrets we share,
Writing our saga, a love affair.

From laughter to tears, the words intertwine,
A tapestry woven, our hearts align.
Beyond the horizon, new tales ignite,
The pages of life, forever in sight.

With every choice, a new path we find,
In the book of our lives, our hearts combined.
Each moment cherished, like ink on a page,
The story of us, a timeless stage.

And when we look back on the lines we've penned,
In the book of our love, may it never end.
For the pages turn, but the tale remains,
A story of joy, through pleasure and pains.

Echoing Paths of Gentle Understanding

In the quiet moments, truth softly speaks,
Through the silent valleys, where the heart seeks.
With every encounter, a chance to embrace,
In echoing paths, we find our place.

In whispers of calm, our thoughts intertwine,
With empathy blooming, like flowers in line.
We tread together on trails yet explored,
In the warmth of compassion, our spirits restored.

Through each shared story, our souls connect,
In the garden of thought, we nurture respect.
With open hearts, we uncover the way,
In echoing paths, we choose to stay.

In moments of doubt, we find strength anew,
Through the shared silence, we create the view.
In gentle understanding, no words need to fall,
In the echo of presence, we embrace it all.

And when the day fades into the night,
In the bond of our hearts, we find our light.
With every step forward, we learn to believe,
In echoing paths, together we achieve.

The Horizon Where Hearts Align

At dawn's first light, dreams begin to rise,
Painting the canvas of azure skies.
With every heartbeat, we chase the sun,
In the horizon's glow, our journey's begun.

With every whisper of the softening breeze,
We gather our hopes, like leaves from the trees.
In the dance of moments, we're quick to find,
The horizon glimmers, where hearts align.

Through valleys of shadows, we wander and roam,
In the warmth of togetherness, we feel at home.
With every step forward, dreams intertwine,
On the horizon's edge, our souls gently shine.

As twilight descends, painting colors anew,
In the tapestry woven, it's me and you.
In the silence of night, dreams bloom and intertwine,
For in the horizon's embrace, our hearts gently align.

With stars as our guide, we journey afar,
Through the tapestry woven, we find who we are.
In love's sweet reflection, where destinies bind,
On the horizon of dreams, our hearts are aligned.

The River of Supportive Streams

In the quiet flow we lean,
Carried by waters velvety sheen,
Messages soft like petals drift,
In currents strong, we find our gift.

Each ripple brings a gentle touch,
Reminding us we are more than much,
Together we sail, wide and free,
In this river, you and me.

Beneath the surface, secrets play,
In shades of blue, they find their way,
A harmony wrapped in embrace,
In supportive streams, we find our place.

With every bend, we learn and grow,
Navigating life's ebb and flow,
We trust the path, we trust the dream,
Together forever, a loyal team.

As twilight glimmers on the tide,
In the river, we can confide,
With every wave, we speak our truth,
To the river, we owe our youth.

Horizons Painted with Heartbeats

Across the sky, the colors blend,
Where time and love gracefully spend,
Each heartbeat echoes in the air,
A canvas crafted with tender care.

Morning brings its golden sigh,
As hopes and dreams begin to fly,
Strokes of passion, vibrant and bright,
Illuminated by the soft twilight.

In shadows cast by love's embrace,
We find the strength to face each space,
The horizon whispers sweet and low,
With every sunset, our spirits glow.

A dance of colors, feelings collide,
Where laughter flows and fears subside,
Our hearts become the artist's hand,
Painting life across this land.

In the twilight, dreams renew,
With every heartbeat, we live true,
Horizons stretch as far as we choose,
In this painted world, we'll never lose.

The Stillness Between Our Whispers

In the hush where secrets dwell,
Soft words linger, casting a spell,
A silence drapes like evening mist,
In that stillness, love coexists.

Breath of moments shared in peace,
Where conversations gently cease,
Our eyes connect, stories unfold,
In quiet chambers, we are bold.

Echoes swirl like leaves in flight,
In this silence, our hearts ignite,
Words unspoken, yet deeply known,
In stillness, our affection's shown.

Between the whispers, we find grace,
A sacred bond in this soft space,
With each heartbeat, a promise sworn,
In silence, true love is reborn.

So let the world around us fade,
In this stillness, we lie unafraid,
For every pause, every breath we share,
Is a testament to the love we bear.

Threads of Connection Weaving Time

In the tapestry of days gone by,
Threads of connection never lie,
Each moment stitched with care and grace,
In the fabric of life, we find our place.

With every laugh, a thread is spun,
Binding hearts, two become one,
In the loom of memories bright,
We weave together, day and night.

Colors blend, and patterns form,
In the warmth, we feel the storm,
Through trials faced, through love's embrace,
With every stitch, we find our space.

The seasons change, yet we hold tight,
In the weave, we find our light,
Each thread a story, old and new,
In this pattern, we start anew.

Time may pass, but we remain,
Intertwined through joy and pain,
In the tapestry that's yours and mine,
We are the threads that weave through time.

Caressing the Edges of Time

In whispered winds, we find a trace,
Echoes of moments, soft and lace.
Time bends gently, like a sigh,
Unraveling dreams that fly so high.

A dance of shadows, light entwined,
Each second valued, love defined.
Memories linger, shadows cast,
Holding the futures, shaped from the past.

Stars above in silent cheer,
Marking the paths we hold so dear.
With every tick, our hearts align,
Caressing the edges, sweet divine.

Moments like pearls, strung in a line,
Glimmers of hope in a world benign.
Embraced in time, we bloom and fade,
In this vast tale, joy is made.

Discovering Hidden Paths of Kindness

Winding roads beneath the trees,
Where whispered kindness rides the breeze.
Hearts connect in gentle ways,
Illuminating darker days.

A smile shared, a helping hand,
These simple acts, like grains of sand.
They build a fortress, strong and bright,
Creating warmth in the coldest night,

In every corner, kindness grows,
Where patience lingers, love bestows.
We find the strength in small embrace,
As hearts unite, we find our place.

Through valleys deep and mountains high,
We find our song, a hopeful sigh.
Where kindness blooms, our spirits soar,
In hidden paths, we find much more.

The Journey of Hearts Aligned

Two souls wandering, hands entwined,
In the chaos, peace we find.
With every step, a tale unfolds,
Promises shared, like whispers bold.

Under starlit skies, we dream,
Following the softest beam.
Hearts aligned, a rhythm sweet,
In every heartbeat, we complete.

Through twisted trails and open fields,
To time's embrace, our fate it wields.
With laughter ringing through the air,
Together always, unaware.

Each chapter written in the stars,
Mapping love, no space for scars.
In this journey, hand in hand,
Hearts aligned, forever stand.

A Chronicle of Gentle Persistence

In quiet corners, strength is found,
Where whispers grow, and dreams abound.
With every setback, we rise anew,
In the dance of life, we push on through.

The road may twist, the storms may roar,
But gentle persistence opens every door.
With every bruise, we learn to soar,
Finding our power, we become more.

Through shadows long, in struggle's grip,
A flame persists, it will not slip.
With courage stitched in every seam,
We walk the path of every dream.

In the tapestry of hopes entwined,
We weave our stories, hearts aligned.
A chronicle written, brave and true,
Of gentle persistence, me and you.

Heartstrings Tied in Harmony

In a world where echoes sigh,
Two hearts beat, no need to try.
Melodies weave in soft embrace,
Together we find our sacred place.

Each note a whisper, pure and sweet,
In every rhythm, our souls meet.
Bound by love, the music flows,
In harmony, our spirit grows.

Through valleys deep and mountains high,
Our song will soar, we'll touch the sky.
In whispered dreams, our futures gleam,
As heartstrings tie, we live the dream.

With every step, we dance as one,
In twilight's glow, our journey's begun.
The world around fades into night,
But hand in hand, we shine so bright.

Together we'll face the coming dawn,
Through every phase, we'll carry on.
A symphony of love, forever true,
In heartstrings tied, it's me and you.

Footprints Left on Paths of Affection

On sandy shores, our footprints blend,
Each step taken, a love to send.
Waves wash over the dreams we trace,
In every mark, a warm embrace.

Through fields of flowers, side by side,
In laughter and joy, our hearts abide.
The path we walk with gentle grace,
Leaves trails of love in every space.

When storms may come, and shadows fall,
Our footprints guide through it all.
Each memory shared, a light so bright,
Guiding us through the darkest night.

In silent whispers of the trees,
Our love, a compass in the breeze.
With every step, we proudly tread,
A journey woven, like words unsaid.

So let us walk, while stars align,
Through paths of affection, yours and mine.
Together creating a lasting line,
Where hearts unite, a love divine.

The Atlas of Empathic Bonds

In every gaze, a map unfolds,
An atlas rich with tales retold.
From mountains high to valleys wide,
In empathic bonds, we take our stride.

Each line a story, deeply sown,
In hearts where kindness has been grown.
Through every chapter, we learn and share,
Navigating life with utmost care.

In whispers of truth, we find our way,
With open hearts, come what may.
The symphony of souls aligns,
In the map of love, our spirit shines.

With courage drawn from each embrace,
We journey onward through time and space.
The true north guides where feelings flow,
In bonds of empathy, we truly grow.

So let us chart these paths of grace,
In the atlas of love, we find our place.
Together we'll explore the vast unknown,
For in every bond, we are not alone.

Radiance in the Journey of Us

In the dawn's light, our dreams take flight,
With every heartbeat, we feel so right.
Through winding roads and skies of blue,
Radiance glows in all we do.

With laughter brightening the darkest days,
Together we dance through life's maze.
Each step we take, a stride in trust,
In the journey of us, it's love we must.

Hand in hand, through thick and thin,
In this together, we always win.
Every challenge met, a chance to shine,
With you beside me, all's divine.

With each sunset, our stories blend,
In twilight's glow, love will extend.
A journey crafted, hearts entwined,
In radiance, forever in mind.

So here we stand, as stars align,
In the journey of us, our hearts combine.
Together we'll write a tale of trust,
In every moment, it's love that's just.

To the End of the Heart's Horizon

Beneath the sky where dreams take flight,
   Whispers of hope, painting the night.
A journey beckons, love's sweet call,
   We chase the light, we stand so tall.

Across the seas, where shadows play,
   Guided by stars, we find our way.
Each step we take, with courage bold,
     Unfolds a tale of love retold.

Together we travel, hand in hand,
   Forging our path on shifting sand.
With every heartbeat, the horizon glows,
In the warmth of knowing, our passion flows.

Through valleys deep and mountains high,
   Our spirits soar, we touch the sky.
With every sunrise, new dreams ignite,
To the end of the heart's horizon, we unite.

In the tapestry of time we'll weave,
   Moments cherished, never to leave.
In laughter and tears, we'll always find,
   The beauty of love, forever entwined.

The Realm of Shared Kindness

In a world where hearts can mend,
A touch of love, a gentle friend.
With open arms, we build a space,
In the realm of kindness, we embrace.

A smile exchanged can light the day,
In simple words, our worries sway.
Through acts of grace, we plant the seeds,
Where compassion grows and hope proceeds.

Together we rise, lifting the weak,
In the beauty of kindness, we seek.
The warmth of support can heal the soul,
Creating a haven, making us whole.

In laughter shared and burdens eased,
In unity's strength, we find our peace.
With every gesture, a bond refined,
In this realm of kindness, hearts aligned.

So let us be beacons, shining bright,
Spreading our love, igniting the light.
In the realm of shared kindness, we find,
A world transformed, with hearts intertwined.

Emotive Echoes Across Distance

In the silence where our voices dwell,
Memories linger, casting a spell.
Though miles apart, our hearts entwine,
In the echoes of love, the stars align.

Whispers of laughter, carried by air,
In the gentle breeze, I feel you there.
With every heartbeat, a song we share,
Emotive echoes, a bond so rare.

Time bends and sways, yet love remains,
In the rhythm of life, through joys and pains.
Across the distances, our souls connect,
In the dance of memories, we reflect.

With every sunset, the shadows fade,
But in our hearts, the love won't evade.
In twilight's glow, we find our way,
Emotive echoes guide us each day.

So let us treasure this timeless grace,
In the distance, find our sacred space.
Through the echoes of love, forever we'll rove,
In each fleeting moment, we discover our grove.

The Dance of Two Souls in Tandem

In the glow of twilight, two shadows sway,
A dance of two souls, come what may.
With every movement, a story told,
In the rhythm of love, we break the mold.

Hand in hand, we glide through the night,
With laughter and whispers, hearts take flight.
Every twirl is a promise made,
In this dance of life, our fears allayed.

Against the backdrop of starlit skies,
We find our harmony in each other's eyes.
In the melody of dreams, we intertwine,
Together we flourish, our spirits align.

With every heartbeat, our spirits ignite,
In the warmth of connection, everything feels right.
As we sway to the music, the world fades away,
In the dance of two souls, forever we stay.

So let the world watch, let the night unfold,
In this dance of love, let our hearts be bold.
Through every stumble, every graceful bend,
We dance as one, lovers until the end.

Horizons of Devotion Explored

Beneath the golden dawn we rise,
Eyes set upon the endless skies.
Each step we take, hearts entwined,
In the beauty of love, we're defined.

Through valleys low and mountains high,
With every whisper, every sigh.
Our journey charts the stars above,
In each horizon, a promise of love.

The winds may blow, the storms may call,
Together we'll stand, refusing to fall.
With hands held tight, we wander far,
Forever guided by our own star.

With each dawn's light, a new day to find,
The secrets of hearts that intertwine.
In the rhythm of life, we will dance,
Our devotion grows with each fleeting chance.

As shadows stretch in evening's glow,
In the warmth of love, we'll always know,
Horizons beckon with tales to unfold,
In the embrace of our hearts, pure and bold.

The Soft Echo of Togetherness

In quiet moments, whispers sigh,
A melody only we can tie.
With every laugh, a song is made,
In the soft echo, memories laid.

Under starlit skies, dreams take flight,
Together we dance through the night.
The world fades away when you're near,
In your presence, all doubts disappear.

Time may rush, but we stand still,
Bound by a love, unbroken will.
Through gentle breezes, our hearts blend,
In the soft echoes, love will mend.

With every tear, a story shared,
A promise kept, a heart laid bare.
In the silence between our hearts' beat,
Lives the tender touch of love complete.

Together we weave a tapestry bright,
Threaded by dreams, shining with light.
In the soft echo, forever we'll stay,
Holding each other, come what may.

Navigating the Currents of Affection

In the river of time, we gently flow,
Navigating currents, love's gentle glow.
With every wave that rocks the shore,
Our bond grows stronger, forevermore.

In whispers shared beneath the moon,
Hearts united like a timeless tune.
Through playful tides, we laugh and sail,
In the depths of care, we'll never pale.

With every storm that challenges fate,
Together we face, we'll never be late.
For love's compass points true and clear,
Guiding our hearts, erasing all fear.

In the stillness where serenity lies,
With open hearts, we touch the skies.
Navigating storms, we find our way,
In the ocean of love, forever we'll stay.

Treading the waters of life's endless sea,
With love as our map, boundless and free.
Hand in hand, we'll embrace the unknown,
In the glow of affection, never alone.

A Chorus of Tender Hearts

In harmony, our voices rise,
A chorus sung beneath the skies.
Each note a promise, soft and sweet,
A symphony where lovers meet.

With gentle chords, our spirits blend,
In this melody, true hearts mend.
With every rhythm, our love ignites,
A dance that sways through starry nights.

In the quiet spaces, we shall find,
The echoes of love, perfectly blind.
Together creating a song so rare,
A chorus sung with tender care.

Through trials faced and joys embraced,
In this sweet song, we have our place.
With laughter, tears, a shared refrain,
In the chorus of hearts, we'll remain.

As the seasons change, our tune will grow,
In this life's concert, love's steady flow.
Together we sing, never apart,
A chorus of love, a lyrical heart.

The Thread of Connection Woven Strong

In whispers light as morning dew,
We weave our dreams, both old and new.
The tapestry of hearts entwined,
A bond of love, forever kind.

Through trials faced, we stand as one,
In shadows cast by setting sun.
Each thread a story, rich and bold,
In warmth of trust, our souls unfold.

With hands held tight, we face the storm,
In unity, we find our form.
Together bright, we shine like stars,
Our hearts aligned, no matter how far.

Life's fabric shifts, yet we remain,
In every joy, in every pain.
The thread that binds, it will not break,
For in this love, we find our wake.

And as the seasons turn and flow,
Our love a garden, ever grow.
In every hue, in every song,
The thread of connection woven strong.

Sails Set on the Sea of Understanding

With winds of grace, our sails take flight,
To explore horizons glowing bright.
On currents deep, our spirits glide,
In waters vast, where truth may bide.

Through storms we navigate with care,
A compass set, our hearts laid bare.
Each wave a lesson, calm or rough,
In depths of trust, we find enough.

The anchor drops where kindness grows,
In gentle tides, our friendship flows.
No shores unseen can keep us from,
The shores of love where we are home.

The sailcloth stitched of hopes and dreams,
Together strong as daylight beams.
In every journey, near and far,
We chart our course, our guiding star.

With every breath, we seek to learn,
In the sea of life, for which we yearn.
Set sails with trust, let waves be free,
On the sea of understanding, you and me.

The Gentle Unfolding of Wants

In garden soft, where wishes grow,
Each petal whispers, soft and slow.
The breeze carries dreams on its wings,
In gentle rhythm, the heart sings.

With tender hands, we shape our fate,
As blooms arise, we cultivate.
Desires sprout in sunlight's gaze,
In quiet moments, love's warm blaze.

The unfolding petals, velvety sweet,
In every longing, our souls meet.
With patience, we let our visions thrive,
In blooms of hope, we come alive.

In silence shared, our hearts awake,
Each yearning spark, a path we make.
From seeds of trust, we sow our dreams,
In gentle moments, life redeems.

As blossoms fade and seasons change,
Our wants transform, yet remain strange.
With every cycle, new paths we find,
In the gentle unfolding, love's unconfined.

Whirls of Timeless Devotion

In circles spun, our souls entwined,
In every gaze, true love defined.
Through echoes vast, our spirits dance,
In whirls of time, we take our chance.

With every spin, the world unfolds,
In quiet moments, our warmth holds.
A rhythm soft, in heartbeat's sway,
In timeless devotion, we find our way.

The universe sings a sacred tune,
In silver light of the glowing moon.
Our dreams align, no distance far,
In whirls of devotion, we are the star.

In every glance, a promise made,
In love's embrace, we're not afraid.
For in the spiral, we're forever bound,
In whirls of timeless love, we're found.

With every step, we leave a trace,
In dances shared, we find our place.
Through all of time, our spirits soar,
In whirls of devotion, forevermore.

The Map of Starlit Devotion

In the night, our dreams take flight,
Like constellations burning bright.
Every whisper, a guiding star,
Charting paths to who we are.

With every heartbeat, a spark ignites,
Illuminating our shared delights.
A canvas woven by fate's design,
Our souls entwined, steadfast, divine.

Through the silence, our hearts converse,
In the universe, we find our verse.
Hand in hand, we journey far,
Together beneath the evening's spar.

Each memory a piece of art,
Treasured tokens of the heart.
In the dark, our love shall steer,
Navigating through doubt and fear.

For in this map, we find our place,
Forever held in love's embrace.
With starlit paths, we shall explore,
A bond that time cannot ignore.

Beneath the Canopy of Togetherness

Under the trees, we softly sway,
In nature's arms, we find our way.
Leaves whisper secrets in the breeze,
Moments captured, hearts at ease.

Sunlight dances on our skin,
Together, we embrace the din.
Laughter shared among the shade,
In this haven, love won't fade.

Each branch above, a shelter grand,
Holding close, we take our stand.
Roots entwined beneath the ground,
A unity in silence found.

As shadows stretch and daylight fades,
In twilight's glow, our hopes cascade.
Every glance, a silent vow,
Beneath the canopy, here and now.

With every step, our spirits rise,
In every heartbeat, love replies.
Together, we face life's long quest,
In unity, we find our rest.

Blossoms of Unseen Care

In the garden where kindness grows,
Unseen efforts, a gentle prose.
Petals soft, like whispered grace,
Hidden treasures take their place.

A nod, a smile, a soft embrace,
Acts of love that time won't erase.
Through the thorns, our spirits bloom,
Filling hearts with sweet perfume.

In the quiet, a friend's support,
Lifelines drawn in every art.
Though silent, the love we share,
Sprouts a blossom, bright and rare.

We cultivate hope with patient hands,
Nurturing dreams in distant lands.
In the shadows, warmth can rise,
And unseen care wears no disguise.

For every act, both big and small,
Planting seeds that echo call.
In this garden, together we stand,
Tending blossoms, heart in hand.

A Tapestry of Warmth and Light

Woven threads of joy and cheer,
Create a tapestry so dear.
Colors vibrant, stories spun,
A dance of hearts, together as one.

In every loop, a memory made,
Of laughter bright in sunshine's glade.
Each stitch a promise, warm and tight,
Embracing shadows, cradling light.

Patterns shift, yet we remain,
Through storms of life, through joy and pain.
Together, we weave solace profound,
In the fabric of love, forever bound.

As threads unite, our spirits soar,
In this artwork, we explore.
In every hue, our hopes ignite,
A tapestry crafted, pure delight.

For in this weave, we find our truth,
A celebration of timeless youth.
With every heartbeat, we grow brighter,
In the tapestry of warmth and light.

The Map of Togetherness

In the quiet space we share,
Lines drawn with gentle care.
Paths woven, side by side,
Through the journey, we abide.

With each step, we find our way,
Guided by the light of day.
Markers of love, bold and true,
Map our lives, just me and you.

No storm can tear our bond apart,
For you've etched within my heart.
A compass made of trust and grace,
In every challenge, we embrace.

Across the hills, the valleys span,
Holding dreams, a shared plan.
Together we'll paint the skies,
With colors that never die.

So here we stand, hand in hand,
In the map of this vast land.
A treasure found, forever clear,
In togetherness, we persevere.

Echoing Through the Valleys of Affection

Whispers float on the evening air,
Carried softly, without a care.
Voices blend in harmony's song,
Echoing love where we belong.

Through the valleys, feelings rise,
Reflections caught in tender eyes.
A melody of hearts that beat,
Resonates in every street.

Soft sighs of warmth, gentle and clear,
In this embrace, we hold so dear.
Let the world fade away tonight,
In the glow of this shared light.

Moments crafted like sculptor's clay,
Molding memories day by day.
With each echo, our love will grow,
In the valleys where feelings flow.

Forever weaving through the night,
Stay with me 'til morning light.
For in our hearts, we've found the way,
Echoing love, come what may.

Silk Threads of Mutual Understanding

Gently woven, threads of gold,
Stories of two, yet to unfold.
In this tapestry, hand in hand,
We find meaning, we take a stand.

Through struggles shared, we learn and grow,
A vibrant dance, the heart's own flow.
With every thread, a bond we tie,
Binding us in love's sweet sigh.

Silk of trust, and friendship's lace,
Stitched together in warm embrace.
Colors shining, bright and bold,
Crafting tales that never grow old.

Our laughter weaves through every seam,
Filling life with hope and dream.
A story rich with joy and tears,
Silk threads binding through the years.

In every moment, pure and rare,
Resonance floats, suspended air.
A fabric strong, yet light and free,
In mutual understanding, we see.

Echoes of Soft Serenity

In the hush of twilight's grace,
Peace descends, a gentle space.
Whispers weave through the fading light,
Echoes of calm in the night.

Moonlight dances on still waters,
Softly stirring, nature's daughters.
Quiet breaths, hearts intertwined,
Seeking solace, love defined.

The world rests in a tender sigh,
Stars above like dreams fly high.
In the silence, we find our tune,
Underneath the silver moon.

Every heartbeat, every glance,
A shared moment, a silent dance.
In soft echoes, we find our place,
Wrapped in love's warm embrace.

Let the night cradle our dreams,
As the universe softly beams.
In this serenity, hearts agree,
Together, forever, you and me.

A Garden of Silent Messages

In whispers soft, the petals sway,
A language blooms in the light of day.
Each color speaks of tales untold,
In this garden's heart, secrets unfold.

The breeze carries thoughts on its flight,
Gently wrapping dreams, taking flight.
Each fragrant scent, a memory's trace,
In the quiet blooms, find their place.

Beneath the arch of the willow's tear,
I find the echoes of friends so near.
Their laughter drifts on the morning air,
In this silent space, I feel them there.

Time stands still in this tranquil space,
Every moment holds a tender grace.
Nature paints with a brush divine,
In a garden where our souls entwine.

As twilight falls and shadows blend,
Messages linger with each sunset's end.
In the hush, a promise to abide,
In this sacred ground, let's not divide.

The Compass Pointing to You

In the world's vast map, I lose my way,
Yet your light shines bright, guiding each day.
Every turn I take feels truly new,
For my compass always points to you.

Through valleys low and mountains high,
I seek your warmth beneath the sky.
North or south, it's clear and true,
Every step I take leads back to you.

Whispers of wind carry your name,
Fires of dreams, they burn the same.
In the darkest nights, your love shines through,
With every heartbeat, I'm close to you.

The stars above, they dance and play,
Mapping out paths where hearts can stay.
In this journey's rhyme, I see the cue,
Every moment spent is lost in you.

As seasons change and rivers flow,
With every ebb, my heart will know.
No matter the distance, I'll make it through,
For my compass forever points to you.

Cherished Moments in the Time's Flow

In the river of time, we float and drift,
Collecting memories, our treasured gift.
With laughter and tears, we weave the thread,
In the fabric of life, our spirits are fed.

Each tick of the clock holds whispering sighs,
Captured glances and heartfelt goodbyes.
In fleeting seconds, we pause and view,
A mosaic of moments that feels so true.

The echo of laughter below the stars,
Reminds us that love can heal all scars.
From dawn's first light to evening's glow,
Each cherished moment continues to grow.

As sands of time slip through our hands,
We stitch our lives with delicate strands.
In the quiet embrace, we both know,
The beauty of moments in time's flow.

With every heartbeat, our story penned,
In the chapters of life, love has no end.
To the rhythm of time, our hearts will sing,
In cherished moments, forever spring.

Underneath the Stars of Shared Aspirations

Beneath the sky, where dreams take flight,
We gather wishes, in the midnight light.
Stars align in patterns bold,
Whispers of hope in stories told.

With each twinkle, a secret shared,
In the fabric of cosmos, we're both ensnared.
Aligning hearts under the celestial view,
Together we roam, chasing what's true.

In the soft glow of twilight's breath,
We find our depth, far beyond death.
A constellation of plans anew,
Underneath the stars, just me and you.

Faded dreams may sometimes wane,
Yet under this sky, we'll rise again.
For every wish upon a star so blue,
Is a promise held in the night's gentle hue.

We grasp the light that shines so bright,
Emboldened, we journey with pure delight.
In each step forward, we have a clue,
Underneath the stars of shared aspirations.

A Tidal Wave of Caring

In the depth of night, whispers call,
Waves of warmth, they break and fall.
Hearts collide in starlit grace,
A tidal wave, in love's embrace.

Gentle hands and softest sighs,
Caress like wind beneath the skies.
Each heartbeat's pulse, a soothing balm,
Together, in the storm, we're calm.

As oceans swell, our voices blend,
In every word, a love to send.
From shores we rise, to seas we soar,
A tidal wave, forevermore.

With every tide, new stories thrive,
In cherished moments, we arrive.
The moon will guide, the stars will bear,
In the depths of caring, we declare.

In every splash, a promise made,
Through every storm, our love won't fade.
With tides that shift, a dance refined,
A tidal wave, so intertwined.

The Compass of Daily Affection

In the morning light, we find our way,
With guiding words, we greet the day.
A compass true, our hearts align,
In daily affection, love will shine.

Through whispered dreams, our spirits roam,
Each laugh and tear, a cherished home.
A gentle touch, a knowing glance,
The compass spins, and we advance.

Moments shared, like leaves in flight,
With every hug, we hold on tight.
In the map of life, our journeys blend,
The compass points to love, my friend.

Through ups and downs, we navigate,
In each embrace, we elevate.
With every step, together we grow,
The compass guides where love will flow.

In fields of joy, our passions flare,
With every heartbeat, tender care.
In daily affection, sweet and clear,
Our compass spins, forever near.

United in the Dance of Days

In morning's light, we leap and sway,
United in the dance of day.
With every step, a story's spun,
Two souls as one, we've just begun.

The rhythm flows, we laugh and twirl,
In every glance, a secret whirl.
The music plays, our spirits rise,
Each dance a gift beneath the skies.

Through gentle steps, we forge ahead,
In every beat, our hearts are fed.
Together strong, we take the lead,
United in the dreams we breed.

With arms entwined, we chase the light,
Through every shadow, fears take flight.
In harmony, our voices blend,
In the dance of days, love will mend.

As twilight falls, we pause, we sigh,
The day may fade, but love won't die.
United still, through night's embrace,
In the dance of days, we find our place.

Navigating Through Calm and Chaos

Through tranquil seas and tempests wild,
We navigate with hearts so mild.
In calm moments, whispers flow,
In chaos, love starts to grow.

With steady hands, we steer the way,
In every wave, a chance to play.
Through storms that rage and winds that call,
Navigating, we won't fall.

As stars will guide our drifting sail,
In every heartbeat, we prevail.
In quiet nights, we hold on tight,
Through chaos comes our shared light.

With every tide, we find our peace,
A bond that strengthens, never cease.
Through ups and downs, we'll ride the flow,
Navigating through, love will show.

In the dance of fate, our paths entwine,
With every challenge, love will shine.
Through calm and chaos, hand in hand,
Navigating life, a perfect strand.

Rippled Reflections of Affection

In quiet pools we find our spark,
Glimmers dance, igniting the dark.
With whispered thoughts and gentle grace,
Our hearts entwined in this sacred space.

Each glance a wave, each touch a sigh,
Echoes of love, as shadows fly.
Beneath the surface, emotions flow,
Rippled reflections of what we know.

In every heartbeat, there's a song,
Melodies crafted, where we belong.
Together we navigate the tide,
With love as our compass, we shall glide.

Moments captured in time's embrace,
A tapestry woven, a warm, soft place.
Through ups and downs, our spirits soar,
Carried on waves, forevermore.

With every heartbeat, our bond refined,
Two souls together, forever intertwined.
In this vast ocean, we rise and fall,
Rippling reflections, uniting us all.

Unfolding Petals of Shared Dreams

In gardens lush, our hopes are sown,
Petals unfold, where love is grown.
With each dawn's light, a new delight,
Together we chase, dreams taking flight.

Through fragrant breezes, whispers soft,
We weave our stories, soaring aloft.
In every color, our hearts align,
Unfolding petals, your hand in mine.

Each moment shared, a fragile bloom,
Radiating warmth, dispelling gloom.
As seasons change, our love persists,
In gardens vast, it's joy we list.

Beneath the stars, we plant our seeds,
Tending our dreams, fulfilling our needs.
Together we flourish, standing tall,
Unfolding petals, we cherish it all.

In twilight's glow, our journey gleams,
Boundless horizons, unending dreams.
Hand in hand, through night and day,
Unfolding petals, love lights the way.

Journeys Beneath the Same Skies

Underneath the vast expanse,
We share our laughter, we share our glance.
Every path we take aligns,
Journeys together, our fate entwines.

Through stormy nights and sunny days,
We navigate life's winding ways.
In every moment, steadfast we stand,
Journeys beneath the same skies, hand in hand.

With every step, memories bloom,
In shadows cast, love finds room.
Stars whisper tales of where we've been,
Guiding our hearts, forever keen.

Across the horizon, dreams await,
With open arms, we build our fate.
In unity, we chase the light,
Journeys beneath the same stars bright.

As twilight kisses the earth goodnight,
We journey onward, hearts alight.
Bound by the skies, our spirits rise,
Together forever, beneath the same skies.

Embracing the Tides of Togetherness

Waves crash gently upon the shore,
As we embrace, longing for more.
The ocean breathes, alive with grace,
In togetherness, we find our place.

With every tide, our hearts align,
In harmony's dance, our souls entwine.
The ebb and flow, a sacred song,
Embracing the tides, where we belong.

Through sunlit days and moonlit nights,
We stand united, facing new heights.
With every challenge, we find our way,
Together we rise, come what may.

As currents shift and change their course,
We hold each other, our steady force.
In the gentle waves, our love will thrive,
Embracing the tides, we come alive.

With whispers soft, we share our dreams,
In this ocean vast, our love redeems.
Hand in hand, we'll face each test,
Embracing the tides, forever blessed.

The Tides of Affection's Reach

Waves whisper secrets to the shore,
Hearts entwined, they seek for more.
Moonlight dances on the sea,
In tides of love, we find our spree.

Gentle breezes carry our dreams,
Beneath the stars, life softly beams.
With every rise, hope finds its way,
In the ocean's heart, we choose to stay.

Shells beneath our feet, they charm,
Each grain of sand, it speaks of calm.
In every tide, affection flows,
In this embrace, our passion grows.

As the sun sinks low in the west,
We hold each moment, feel it's best.
Together we'll weather, come what may,
In tidal love, we choose to play.

Through storms and calm, our bond will cling,
In every season, our hearts take wing.
With steadfast faith, we chart our course,
In the tides of love, we find our source.

Embracing the Unwritten Chapters

Pages turn in life's vast book,
Filled with moments, come take a look.
Words unspoken, yet deeply felt,
In silence, our stories melt.

Hand in hand, we write anew,
In the ink of dreams, find what's true.
The future beckons, a blank decree,
With every heartbeat, you and me.

Unfolding paths before our eyes,
Adventure calls beneath the skies.
In the laughter shared, joy shines bright,
Together we weave, day into night.

Every glance, a verse untold,
With every breath, a treasure gold.
The journey calls; we'll face it strong,
In the embrace of where we belong.

With hope as our lantern, we step ahead,
The unwritten chapters are ours to thread.
In every twist, in every bend,
Together we'll write, till the very end.

Pledges Across Time's Canvas

Brush strokes of time, colors blend,
In each moment, our hearts ascend.
Promises made on the canvas wide,
In the palette of love, we confide.

Each sunset spills vivid hues,
Life's canvas holds both joy and blues.
With every stroke, we lay our claim,
A masterpiece born from passion's flame.

Through shades of doubt and tones of trust,
In the art of love, we find what's just.
With every pledge, we paint our fate,
In the gallery where we create.

Time whispers softly, urging us on,
In the portrait of life, our hearts are drawn.
With every stroke of gentle care,
We weave our dreams in the open air.

Together we flourish, our spirits free,
In the canvas of time, just you and me.
Through every color, our love will show,
In pledges made, forever we'll grow.

The Journey Through Storm and Sunshine

Paths unfurl in harmonic grace,
As we wander, time shouldn't race.
Through storms that roar and sun that beams,
We chase our hopes, we dare to dream.

Raindrops fall, a rhythmic song,
In every challenge, we grow strong.
With laughter bright and hands entwined,
In every heartbeat, love defined.

The sun will break, the skies will clear,
With every moment, we draw near.
Through trials faced and joys we've known,
In the journey's arc, our love has grown.

Adventure waits in each sunrise,
As fears dissolve, we touch the skies.
In every trial, we find the way,
Through storm and sunshine, here we stay.

With every step, we pave the road,
In unity, we share the load.
Together we'll dance, in rain or glow,
Through storm and sunshine, ever we'll go.

Whispers of the Heart's Embrace

In the quiet night, softly we sigh,
Holding dreams close, as moments pass by.
Gentle shadows dance on the wall,
Under the stars, to love we call.

Whispers awaken, secrets so true,
In the warmth of your touch, I feel anew.
Every heartbeat sings a sweet refrain,
Binding our souls in joy and in pain.

Through the silence, your voice finds me clear,
A melody played, only we hear.
Tangled in time, together we stay,
Embraced by the night, drifting away.

Every glance shared, a tender caress,
In the whispers, we find happiness.
Moments we cherish, unwritten yet known,
In each other's hearts, we have grown.

As the dawn breaks, our dreams take flight,
With whispers of love, we greet the light.
In the heart's embrace, forever we'll roam,
Together in whispers, we've found our home.

The Road of Gentle Affection

Upon the path where flowers bloom wide,
We tread with care, with love as our guide.
Sunlight dapples through leaves overhead,
With each gentle step, sweet words are said.

The breeze stirs softly, a soft serenade,
In the hush of the woods, fond memories fade.
Hand in hand, through the shadows we glide,
On the road of affection, we take each stride.

Every season changes, but love remains strong,
With gentle affection, we'll always belong.
Through trials and storms, we'll find our way,
In the glow of your heart, I long to stay.

The road is winding, but never a chore,
With you by my side, I couldn't ask for more.
In the laughter we share, the tears that we've shed,
On the road of affection, our love is our thread.

In the twilight's glow, our journey unfolds,
A tapestry woven with stories retold.
With every sunset, new chapters arise,
On the road of affection, love never dies.

Echoes of Kindred Souls

In the vast expanse where the shadows play,
Echoes linger softly, guiding our way.
Two kindred souls, drawn through the night,
In the whispers of time, we find our light.

Moments collide, like waves on the shore,
In each other's eyes, we find the encore.
With laughter and tears, a rhythm so sweet,
In the echoes of love, our hearts gently meet.

Through valleys of silence, we wander hand in hand,
Kindred spirits, a bond so grand.
Every tender glance, a story retold,
In the echoes of kindness, our hearts unfold.

As the stars align, drawing us near,
Echoes of laughter, we hold so dear.
With each step forward, we journey as one,
In the symphony of souls, our song's just begun.

In the stillness of night, our dreams intertwine,
Echoes of kindred souls, your heart next to mine.
In the dance of fate, we believe and we trust,
In the echoes of love, together we must.

Tidal Waves of Tenderness

In the quiet moments, the tide rolls in,
Waves of tenderness, where dreams begin.
With every ebb, a sweet caress,
In the rhythm of love, we find our rest.

The ocean whispers secrets soft and low,
In the depths of our hearts, this love will flow.
Crashing gently, like hearts that collide,
In the tidal waves, I want you by my side.

Every wave that breaks, brings us closer still,
With the tides of affection, we're under love's thrill.
Finding solace in the swell and retreat,
In this dance of the ocean, our hearts skip a beat.

As the sun sets low, the colors ignite,
Tidal waves of tenderness, painting the night.
With the stars above, our spirits find peace,
In the timeless embrace, all worries release.

Through the storms that may come, we'll stand as one,
Tidal waves of love, under moonlight run.
In the arms of the ocean, forever we'll stay,
Together in this magic, we'll never drift away.

Milton Keynes UK
Ingram Content Group UK Ltd.
UKHW021008061024
449204UK00010B/508